Ray Kroc

Mayor of McDonaldland

by Paul Westman

Illustrated by Mary Molina

DILLON PRESS, INC. MINNEAPOLIS, MINNESOTA

Library of Congress Cataloging in Publication Data

Westman, Paul.
    Ray Kroc, mayor of McDonaldland.

    (Taking Part; 3)
    SUMMARY: A biography of the man whose assembly line methods
of preparing food revolutionized the restaurant business and gave birth to
the McDonald restaurant chain.
    1. Kroc, Ray, 1902- —Juvenile literature.
    2. Restaurateurs—United States—biography—Juvenile literature.
    [1. Kroc, Ray, 1902- 2. Restaurateurs] I. Title.
    TX910.5.K76W47   338.7'61'64795 [B] [92]   79-19913

ISBN 0-87518-185-6

RAY KROC

As a young man in Chicago, Ray Kroc tried everything from playing the piano in nightclubs to selling Lily cups and Multimixers. Then he came upon an idea which was to revolutionize the restaurant business in America— good-tasting, low-cost fast food. Because Kroc's assembly line methods of preparing food have been so successful, he has been called the "Henry Ford of the hamburger." From his first McDonald's in Des Plaines, Illinois, the fast-food chain grew in ten years into a worldwide company. Hamburgers, shakes, and fries have become a classic American meal.

Oak Park, Illinois, was a fun place for a boy to live. Oak Park was part of Chicago. It had wide, shady streets and nice, neat homes. Model T's and touring cars moved through the streets. With bottles clanking, the milkman's horse and wagon rumbled noisily over the cobblestones.

Raymond Albert Kroc was born in Oak Park on October 5, 1902. He had a little brother named Bob and a little sister named Lorraine.

Ray's father, Louis Kroc, worked for Western Union. Western Union was a large telegraph company. Mr. Kroc had worked there since he was 12 years old. Starting as a messenger boy, he now had a good job in the office. Often Mr. Kroc looked serious. But he had his cheerful side, too. He loved music, and he loved to laugh.

Ray's mother, Rose Kroc, enjoyed music, too. Mr. Kroc belonged to a singing group. Often Mrs. Kroc played piano for the group. She also gave piano lessons for children to bring in extra money.

Mrs. Kroc made sure that Ray learned to play the piano. She gave him lessons and saw to it that he practiced. Ray was a gifted player. Mostly he liked the time he spent at the piano.

But sometimes it seemed to Ray that his mother went too far. He had to practice long hours each week. Often when he was out playing, his mother would come to the door. She would call loudly, "Raymond! It's time for piano!" Then the other boys would try to call him in that same voice. Ray would leave, ashamed.

Mrs. Kroc kept her house neat and clean. All the children helped. Ray swept and scrubbed and made beds. He beat rugs on the clothesline. He did not mind housework. In fact, he liked it. He wanted things to be neat and clean, too.

Ray's grandparents were from Bohemia. They lived near the Krocs. Grandmother kept things even

neater than Mrs. Kroc. Her kitchen floor was sparkling clean. Each week she scrubbed it with hot soapy water. Then she covered it with newspapers for another week. Why? To keep it clean, of course!

Ray was a student at Lincoln Grammar School. But he did not care much for books or reading. He liked doing things better than reading about them.

Still, Ray did a lot of thinking. He thought of things he could do to make money. His mother teased him about this. She called him "Danny Dreamer."

At Lincoln Grammar School, Ray was on the baseball team. He was one of the school's best players. Baseball was his favorite sport. When Ray turned seven, his father began taking him to the ball park. There they watched the Chicago Cubs.

Ray saw many great ball players in action. He learned all he could about the men and their careers.

Ray and his friends played baseball a lot, too. They could not afford new things to play with. Their bat was old and chewed up, and their baseball was bandaged with tape. A garbage can lid served as home base.

Ray was always busy. Once he started a lemonade stand. Later he worked at the soda fountain in his uncle's drugstore. Here he found that he enjoyed selling things. He was always friendly and smiling and people liked to talk to him. Sometimes he could sell a sundae to a customer who had asked for just a cup of coffee.

Ray saved every penny he earned. He hoped to go into business himself one day.

As he grew older, Ray became more and more musical. In church he played the organ. In Boy

Scouts he played the bugle. He kept right on playing the piano, too.

Often Ray visited Chicago's Loop. The Loop was the name for the heart of downtown Chicago. This was where the tall buildings and busy streets were. In the Loop there were large dime stores such as F. W. Woolworth and S. S. Kresge. The dime stores had large music sections which sold sheet music for pianos.

The stores hired men to play the music so that people would know which songs they wanted to buy. Ray listened to these piano men as often as he could. He thought it would be great fun to play piano and make money at the same time.

Ray was in high school now. He still tried to think of ways to make money, and he saved all he earned. One summer Ray and two friends went into the music business. They used their savings to rent a shop and buy goods. In the shop they sold sheet music and instruments.

Ray was the store's piano man. He played and sang what people asked to hear. But the store did poorly. After a few months it was forced to close.

The only thing Ray liked about school was a debate class. He enjoyed speaking before a crowd trying to persuade others to accept his point of view. Otherwise, he thought school was a waste of time.

After two years of high school, Ray dropped out. He felt that he was old enough to make it on his own. Mr. Kroc was upset when Ray quit school. Because his family had been too poor, Mr. Kroc had never finished high school. He wanted his children to have the schooling he had missed.

That summer Ray took a job selling coffee beans door-to-door. At this time many countries in Europe were fighting in the First World War. In 1917 America entered the war. Young men joined the army to fight in France.

Ray wanted to join the army, too. But he was only 15 years old. Still, he wanted to fight very badly. He lied about his age and joined the Red Cross as an ambulance driver.

Ray and some other men went to Connecticut for training. They drilled hard. Ray looked forward to the day he would sail for France on a big troop ship.

At camp Ray made new friends. One boy there was just a little older than Ray. He was very quiet, and a good artist. When the others went to town, he stayed at camp to draw pictures. His name, Ray learned, was Walt Disney.

Just before Ray was going to leave for France, the war ended. He returned to Chicago where he got a job as a salesperson again. In his spare time he played piano for pay. Ray was so good at both jobs that soon he was making more money than his father.

At last he quit his sales job to play jazz piano full time. He played in many different bands. One place he played was a ballroom called the Edgewater. There Ray met a girl named Ethel Fleming. Later they were married.

To make more money, Ray got a job selling paper cups for the Lily Cup Company. He sold the cups to restaurants and drugstores.

Paper cups were new then, but he found that he could not make a living selling them. He took a second job at a radio station, WGES. Radio was new then, too, and stations were small. WGES broadcast from the Oak Park Arms Hotel. Because WGES was so small, Ray had many chores. He played the piano, chose music, and hired acts.

One night a comedy team named Sam and Henry came in. Since they were looking for work, Ray watched their act. Sam and Henry sang songs and told jokes. Ray hired them. Later Sam and Henry changed the name of their act to Amos and Andy. Amos and Andy became famous radio stars.

With two jobs, Ray was very busy. He worked from seven in the morning until two at night. That left him little time for sleep.

In 1925 a land boom hit Florida. Thousands of people went south to buy land. Ray traveled to Florida, too, but he didn't go to buy land. He wanted a job selling it.

Ray got a job with a land company and quickly became one of the best salespersons on the force. He was making more money than ever. Then, after just a few months, hard times hit Florida. Land prices dropped. Ray was out of work.

To make ends meet, he took a job playing piano in a nightclub. Soon Ray and Ethel grew homesick. Ethel and their young daughter, Marilyn, went back to Chicago by train.

Ray left Florida in the middle of winter. Driving an open Model T, he went straight through to Chicago. He stopped only to pull off the road to sleep. As he traveled north, the weather grew colder and colder. By the time Ray reached Chicago, he was freezing cold—and broke.

Soon Ray had his old job back. The company was

19

called Lily-Tulip now. He put all his energy into selling cups. No more piano playing or odd jobs for him.

Ray worked harder than ever. He sold cups all over Chicago. He sold to shops, restaurants, drugstores, beaches, zoos, and ball parks.

Then he had an idea. He began selling to big places that needed hundreds of cups. That way he could make more sales with less work. When the cups were gone, the companies would have to renew their orders.

Ray sold to large drugstore chains. He sold to big companies with large lunchrooms where hundreds of workers ate. Ray Kroc was the best salesperson at Lily-Tulip. Soon he had fifteen salespeople and a secretary working for him. Kroc was put in charge of all Midwest sales.

While selling cups he met a man named Earl Prince. Prince had invented a machine called the Multimixer. The Multimixer was a milk shake mixer. Instead of mixing one shake, like other mixers, it mixed six—all at the same time.

This machine excited Kroc. He and Prince became partners in a new business. Prince made the machines, and Kroc sold them.

At first it was not easy. Most owners already had small mixers. Also, they were afraid the Multimixer might break down. If one of their small mixers broke down, it did not matter. They just switched to another one. But if a big mixer broke down, they could not make any shakes at all. This did not stop Ray Kroc. He kept selling, and slowly sales increased.

Then came World War II and a copper shortage. Earl Prince could not build mixers because there was no copper for the motors.

After the war Kroc began selling mixers again. Sales were good. Traveling all over the country, he saw hundreds of restaurants and ice cream stands. Kroc sold his mixers to such chains as Dairy Queen, Tastee Freeze, and A&W Root Beer.

In his travels he noticed many things about restaurants. Some restaurant kitchens were clean. Others were sloppy. Some kitchens made good-tasting food. Others made food that tasted bad. Some kitchens gave fast service, while others were slow.

Soon Kroc was an expert on restaurants. Just by looking, he could tell which ones would succeed and which ones would fail.

In 1954 Kroc heard about two brothers named Maurice and Dick McDonald. They owned a restaurant in San Bernardino, California. At that time San Bernardino was a little town on the edge of the Mojave Desert.

Kroc was amazed to learn that the McDonalds owned eight Multimixers. He wondered what kind of place would need to make 48 shakes at once. To find out, Kroc flew to California. Early one morning he drove out to the McDonald's stand.

It was small and clean. On the roof was a large sign. It said, "McDonald's Famous Hamburgers, 15¢—Buy 'Em By the Bag."

Soon workers arrived dressed in white shirts, white pants, and white paper hats. They went to a building behind the stand and took out supplies to bring into the restaurant. Kroc watched them carry cartons of meat, sacks of potatoes, and boxes full of buns, pop, and milk.

The parking lot began to fill with cars. People formed long lines at the windows. Kroc was amazed. Never had he seen a restaurant do so much business. He knew he had to meet the McDonald brothers.

Maurice and Dick were from New Hampshire. In 1927 they had moved to California. First they

worked for a movie studio. Before long they ran their own movie house. Finally they bought a drive-in restaurant. The brothers made a good living from it. But one day in 1948, they had a new idea. They decided to try something that had never been done before.

The McDonalds threw out their old menu and started selling nothing but hamburgers, french fries, and milk shakes. They made their food on a type of assembly line. It tasted good and did not cost much.

People began flocking to the McDonald's stand. They told their friends how good the food was, and the friends told their friends. Soon McDonald's was famous in and around San Bernardino.

Kroc was excited by what he saw. He dreamed of hundreds of McDonald's stands dotting the land, instead of just one in San Bernardino. He thought of all the Multimixers he could sell to them. Why, he might become a millionaire!

The next day he returned to the stand. He watched the whole process over again. This time he watched closely to see how the food was made.

27

Kroc paid most attention to the french fry cook. The McDonald brothers made the best french fries he had ever tasted. They were thin, light, and golden brown. People bought bag after bag of them.

McDonald's french fries were made from the best Idaho potatoes. The potatoes were peeled to leave just a thin layer of skin. Then they were sliced into fries.

The raw fries were dumped into a big sink of cold water. The french fry cook plunged his arms into the water and stirred it around. The water grew white with starch.

Next the fries were taken from the sink and rinsed. After that they were placed in wire baskets and cooked in hot oil. This gave them just the right flavor.

Later, Kroc told the McDonalds about his idea and asked them to open a chain modeled after their San Bernardino restaurant. He promised to sell them Multimixers to put in all the hamburger stands.

"But we don't want to open more places,"

Maurice said. "That would be too much work. We are making money now. All we want is to enjoy life, to take it easy."

Kroc thought fast. "Why don't you get someone else to open them for you?" he asked.

"Yes, but who could we find?" Dick asked.

"Well," Kroc said, "how about me?"

Maurice and Dick agreed. Kroc and the McDonalds became partners. Ray Kroc set to work eagerly to make McDonald's a success.

In 1955 Kroc opened his first McDonald's in Des Plaines, Illinois. Des Plaines was near Chicago.

Kroc planned to spend part of his time in Chicago and part in Des Plaines. He would work both at McDonald's and at his job selling Multimixers.

The Des Plaines building was made of red and white tile with big windows on the front and sides. Two yellow arches passed through the roof. This drive-in would serve as a model for all the others.

Business was brisk from the start. Crowds of people flocked to McDonald's in Des Plaines, just

as they had in San Bernardino. McDonald's was something new. Never before had there been a drive-in or restaurant like it.

Kroc was pleased by his drive-in's success. Each morning he drove from Chicago to Des Plaines to open for the day. Then he returned to the city by train. In the evening he was back in Des Plaines once more.

Kroc made sure that his McDonald's was spotlessly clean. Even though he was the owner, he was not too proud to help clean up. Often he swept or mopped around the parking lot and building.

He returned to Des Plaines each day about dusk. As he walked over from the railway station, the light would be fading from the sky. Ray was always thrilled to see his McDonald's come into view. Its neon lights and yellow arches glowed brightly.

Soon Kroc set to work opening other McDonald's restaurants. He picked many of the new sites himself. They had to be chosen carefully so that they would not lose money.

Kroc went to the suburbs of cities to search for

places with tree-lined streets and nice homes. Then he flew over the sites in a light plane. From the plane he counted the number of church steeples and street corners he saw. This told him which sections had many families and where the most traffic was.

Within a few years Kroc had opened more than two hundred outlets. But he and the McDonald brothers were no longer friends. In 1961 Kroc bought them out. From that time on he was the sole owner of McDonald's.

One thing about the sale angered him. The McDonald brothers had agreed to sell their San Bernardino drive-in to Kroc. At the last minute they refused to do so. Kroc needed the extra money it would bring. He felt the brothers had gone back on their word.

The brothers renamed their restaurant The Big M. No longer did they have the right to use their own name on the building. Kroc was still mad about what they had done. He opened a shiny new McDonald's right across the steet from the Big M. He ran the Big M out of business.

Still, Maurice and Dick were millionaires. They retired to Palm Springs and traveled. Ten years later Maurice died, and Dick moved back to New Hampshire.

Now that Kroc owned the business, he was free to run it as he saw fit. The McDonald brothers had come up with the fast-food idea. But they had done nothing to make it grow. Ray Kroc had done that. He was the one who had made McDonald's a big success.

In the 1960s McDonald's grew from a small chain into a large business. It grew faster than almost any other company in America. People liked the food McDonald's served. Hamburgers, shakes, and fries became a classic American meal. They tasted good and didn't cost much for a family to eat.

From Maine to California, every McDonald's was the same. Each one sold the same food, in the same style buildings, and at the same prices. People knew what to expect when they ate at McDonald's.

McDonald's hired many high school students to work in its restaurants. Students were good workers.

Unlike adults, they could work for a few hours each day and on weekends. Many young people found work who would not have been able to get jobs elsewhere.

Ray Kroc learned neatness from his mother while

still a boy in Oak Park. As head of McDonald's, he required every outlet to be kept clean.

Once he walked into a McDonald's in Canada. The iron railing was rusty. The fences needed paint. The floor was dirty.

"Get someone to mop this floor at once," Kroc said to the manager. "If you don't, I'll do it myself!"

The manager did not need to be told twice. He got the floor mopped.

McDonald's became so big that it spread to every major city in the United States. Many who joined the company in its early days became rich. McDonald's built an eight-story headquarters building in Oak Brook, Illinois. To train people to run its restaurants, it set up a place called Hamburger University.

Hamburger University was in Elk Grove, Illinois. Anyone who wanted to run a McDonald's had to take lessons there. Students were taught how to make hamburgers and french fries, buy food, and keep books. They learned all about the hamburger business from top to bottom.

At each McDonald's food was made in an assembly line style. Each person had a special job to do. Lights on the grills told just the right time to flip the meat. A computer measured how long french fries should be cooked. Warming lights kept cooked food warm until it was served. Most orders were filled as soon as people gave them.

McDonald's hamburgers were all the same weight, thickness, and size. The same amount of ketchup, mustard, and pickles was put on each bun.

For a long time McDonald's sold nothing but hamburgers, shakes, fries, and pop. But as time went on, new foods were added.

The idea for the Filet-O-Fish sandwich came from a McDonald's in Cincinnati, Ohio. Cincinnati had many Catholics. At that time Catholics could not eat meat on Fridays. Each Friday the McDonald's owner lost business. He lost so much business that he was afraid he would have to close down.

McDonald's test kitchen in Illinois worked to find an answer. Since Catholics could eat fish on Fridays,

the kitchen decided to make a fish sandwich. It ran tests to find out what kind of fish to use, how long to cook it, and how thick it should be. Many other problems were worked out as well.

But the final touch was not made in the test kitchen. It was made by a young McDonald's worker. One day the worker decided to have a fish sandwich. Before eating it, he added a slice of cheese. That is how the final touch was added to McDonald's Filet-O-Fish.

One new McDonald's burger was an instant success all over America. This was the Big Mac. Instead of a plain hamburger, it had two beef patties, three buns, lettuce, onions, pickles, special sauce, and a slice of cheese.

Later a breakfast item, the Egg McMuffin, was invented. It was made with a fried egg, a piece of cheese, and a slice of Canadian bacon. These were all served on a toasted English muffin.

McDonald's also added a large order of french fries, the Shamrock Shake, the Quarter Pounder, hot apple pie, and other items.

But not all the new ideas worked. One that did not was the Hulaburger. This was a slice of grilled pineapple and two pieces of cheese on a bun. The only thing wrong with the Hulaburger was that no one bought it.

In 1966 McDonald's All-American High School Band was formed. The band was made up of the two best high school band members from every state in the Union. Each year the McDonald's Band marched in the big Macy's Thanksgiving Day parade in New York City.

Ronald McDonald, the company clown, first appeared in the Thanksgiving Day parade that year. Ronald's funny face became well known to children across the land.

Actually, there was more than one Ronald McDonald. In fact, there were fifty Ronald McDonalds around the country. They appeared at parades, county fairs, and grand openings. In Hollywood there was a special Ronald McDonald. This Ronald made all of the company's TV commercials.

By now McDonald's was a worldwide company. The yellow arches glowed brightly in almost every city in the country. There were McDonald's restaurants in London, Paris, and Tokyo. All over the world people ate McDonald's hamburgers.

Ray Kroc had worked hard during his life. He had not met the McDonald brothers until 1954, when he was 52 years old. Now he was a millionaire many times over. He had lots of money, and the time to enjoy it. And that is just what he did.

Ray bought a big ranch in California. He bought four helicopters and a private yacht. He drove a Rolls Royce.

Ray also bought a mansion in Florida. The doorbell of the mansion chimed the McDonald's tune, "You Deserve a Break Today." He had the golden arches symbol set in jewels on his luggage, his cuff links, his rings, and his tie clips. He even had the

arches stitched onto the pockets of his blazers.

Yes, Ray Kroc was rich and famous. But he had not changed all that much. Many evenings he spent at home, playing jazz tunes on his grand piano. Ray could not stand people who put on airs. His favorite meal was McDonald's hamburgers. And he still loved baseball as much as ever.

In fact, he liked baseball so much that he decided to buy a team of his own. First he tried to buy the Chicago Cubs, but the owner would not sell. So, in 1974, Kroc bought the San Diego Padres instead. "I bought this team to have fun," Kroc said.

But Kroc did not spend money just on himself. He also gave a great deal of it away.

When McDonald's needed a company plane, Kroc bought it. It was a jet, and he paid more than $4 million for it. He let the company use it at a charge of $1 per year.

Kroc also bought a fleet of Greyhound buses. The buses had kitchens, telephones, and color TVs. These, too, he rented to the company for $1 per year. McDonald's used them to take poor children and old people on outings, among other things.

Over the years he gave several million dollars to the Kroc Foundation. The Kroc Foundation used the money to try to find cures for diabetes, arthritis, and multiple sclerosis. These diseases cripple and kill many people each year. Often they strike the young. Perhaps someday, with the foundation's help, these diseases will be stopped.

Chicago had always been Kroc's home. He had a special feeling for the city. In 1972, when he turned 70, he decided to do something special for Chicago. He gave more than $7 million to its hospitals,

museums, and churches. He gave $9 million to McDonald's workers, too.

In just 10 years, McDonald's had grown from a single restaurant to one of the biggest companies in the world. Ray Kroc had made it happen. Henry Ford was famous for using the assembly line to make cars. Ray Kroc brought the idea of the assembly line to restaurants. He was the "Henry Ford of the Hamburger."

And in making fast-service common, he changed the diet of a nation—and maybe the world.

"I was a dreamer," Ray Kroc said. "But I was also a doer."

The Author

Paul Westman is a regular contributor to *Current Biography* and has written many books for young people, including several for the Taking Part series. Of the series, Westman says, "Young readers will learn something about well-known contemporary men and women in many challenging fields and at the same time begin to discover some of the joys of reading."

    A recent graduate of the University of Minnesota, Westman lives in Minneapolis.

The Illustrator

Mary Molina is an instructor at the Art Instruction Schools in Minneapolis and a graphic artist for the University of Minnesota Health Service. Her educational background includes the Art Institute of Chicago, the University of California, L'École des Arts Décoratifs, the University of Minnesota, and Furman University.

82-17

MAR 1 3 1992

0

B
KRO

82-17

Westman, Paul

Ray Kroc; mayor of the McDonald-
land